AF365173

Shadowed Souls

an anthology

by

Dortith

First Edition 2017

© 2017 - Dortith

ISBN-13: 978-1543068047
ISBN-10: 1543068049

Publisher: Createspace

For M.J.S.

Shadows

Foreword

This small selection of poems is taken from a collection written
over a period of five decades - a lifetime. Though the poems cover
different topics and feelings there is a similarity of style, theme
and outlook for which 'shadowed' seemed an apt description. They
reflect a view of the world that never truly sees it in the full light
of day. Maybe the mood, subject or words of these poems and
those in the related volumes, will find some echo in the reader's
mind where another self stands in the shadows beside them.

Dortith 2017

Serials for breakfast

They walk and talk
and breathe and stalk
but who has put the breath in them,
who has put the death in them?
They take a life
with gun or knife;
they slink into the night to hide
and with what pride they gloat
and smile over the misery
that they have wrought and the trials
that they have brought into the lives
of innocents, with their hate
and their violence.

How much worse was Sodom's kind
to bear the curse of a dark God's mind?
How much more vile than to kill a child,
that they should be destroyed so utterly,
whilst these are left to wander free
with nothing more than the same God's plea
to "love one another as I have loved thee" ?

2

A Kind of Lost

Some call it lost
that has only been mislaid,
it may be hidden,
perhaps for days,
but it shall be found;
it is not lost.
Some say a thing is lost
when it has slipped silently
from their possession,
dropped and been passed by,
and though finding becomes an obsession
it only lies concealed
in a place where its presence
cannot yet be revealed,
but it is not lost
for Time shall find it out
and it shall come to hand,
perhaps not that from which it parted,
but it is not lost.

Others speak of lost
when someone close,
someone loved,
has merely strayed,
gone their way
to only they know where,
and may for a time,
perhaps a lifetime,
wander a path unfamiliar
to those that wait in despair,
but they are not lost
merely travellers
in a land that's strange
and though never the same
they are not lost.

Then there is another lost,
like affection, respect,
dignity, a friend or lover,
a parent spurned
when bad blood turns
to distance and time elapsed
apart, away, days and years
never to be regained;
that is lost.
A hopeless lost;
like dreams and hopes,
aspirations, nurtured,
held safe and secret,
that fade and vanish,
when no holding,
wanting or needing
can make them true,
can keep them alive;
that is lost.

The lost that acts like acid on the brain,
eating memories, melting self,
the person born inside
that grew and played, and dreamt,
and cried; the one we seemed
so sure we knew,
the one we thought
would always be true,
the one that Time erodes
and wears away, until one day
we look in a mirror and say
I don't know you;
that is lost.

Then there is the absolute lost,
like Time, like years,
like tears of regret,
like joys we forget,
the cost of life paid in full,
the spark of life all spent
before any can tell of its going
or where it went;
a lost so final that words
cannot speak the finding
nor mind conceive again
the seeing, the holding,
possessing, knowing
and even memory cannot hold
for long an image that can mimic
that which is lost,
cannot turn again to gold
the dull lead of reminiscence
no matter how briefly
and tears alone come nearest,
clear, transient, featureless tears,
to recalling that which has so utterly
disappeared, faded, degraded,
vanished, gone,
passed beyond all hope of returning.
That is lost.

Vampyr

Waiting alone in darkness.
In darkness alone can he wait.
For darkness alone must he wait.
A life spent in darkness,
a life spent in waiting;
a life spent,
lived in darkness,
lived in waiting,
spent in the darkness,
the darkness of waiting.
Awaiting Night,
the soul's Night,
darker than any moonless
starless Night to a dark soul,
dark child of the soulless Night.

Night's dark-life is lived in him,
as he lives in the dark-life of Night,
sharing its dark dreams,
dreams of Light,
of Light in darkness;
a dream of Light
that will never shine,
not in his life,
that will not shine,
not in his Night,
that will not brighten his dark,
that cannot lighten his heart
as it cannot lighten his life,
a light that dare not enter
the deep night of his soul.

With the Night he shares
his hopes of Dawn,
shares his dark desire for daylight,
for a day to dawn and end his Night,
for a light to brighten his dark,
a light to pierce his dark-life.
He broods on the pain of that desire,
desire without the delight,
without even the hope of requite;
dwells in the dark agonies
of a soul sinking, sinking,
sinking into darkness,
descending into lightless despair,
the despair of a heart
that knows only Night,
knows only waiting
and the futility of yearning
for a dawn that will never come,
a day that will never dawn,
knowing that to his long night
there is no end, no light,
no tunnel's end to this endless tunnel
of endless night, his Night
that will never end;
this he knows and is crushed
by the knowledge, the knowing
that his heart will never know
the light, the day, the dawn,
the warmth, only the cold,
only the dark, only the Night;
impenetrable dark,
interminable Night.

It is this dark thought,
this lost hope,
this detested desire
that drives his hate,
that feeds his bitterness,
fuels his rage,
rents his dreams,
tears at the fabric
of his dark soul
and breaks his barren heart,
and causes his dark mind to scream
and rage and weep;
that drives the vengeful cruelty
of his dark and vile deeds,
of his darker, viler thoughts,
of his blacker, hateful needs,
of his Stygian, black and hopeless dreams,
dark dreams that come to him
whispering in the darkest silence
of his blackest, lifeless,
lightless Nights.

Beauty and the Beast

And like a child beaten,
bowed his head and wept,
as she, like a beam of light
wandering, sunless, orphaned,
kept from the bright heavens
yet wistful-shining still
went her way and lost to sight
walked on, away from him.

Glistening in the gloom
of an ivied frame,
where spiders weave
in black-leaved rooms
on dusty looms and never sleep
but silent keep in silken webs
their awful watch,
dark eyes unblinking gaze
till the bleeding sun sinks
and the moon rises
through the twilit haze,
into the darkening sky,
like a ruddy scimitar cast
from a remorseful hand
after a fatal duel fought
between the sun and the land;
a blinded eye, opaque and glazed,
suspended in the twilight,
caught in the awful web of Night
and forever lost to the Day.

Then sighs as the shadowed West
becomes one purple vastness
and stark silhouettes dissolve
into a sparkling shroud
as the stars, like faeries
afraid of revelation,
creep from their beds to shed
their cold light on him who weeps
and never sleeps,
he the hated, the feared,
the sorrowing Beast.

The Damned

Imagine a child
lost in a city,
banished from hope,
from love, from pity,
alone in a vast labyrinth
of streets, bazaars
and endless arcades,
filled with faceless,
senseless shades,
all distracted,
wandering sightless,
uncaring not daring to cease
their constant flight.

Shadowed buildings
windows vacant,
looming lightless,
damp hollow spaces
carved into the choking smog.
The groan and screech
of unnerving sounds,
monsters, barely hidden,
half glimpsed, lurking,
waiting, surly eyes watching,
cold hands groping, seeking,
dull feet following
down blind twisting alleys,
narrow and cramped,
reeking of fear;
the stumbling, the weeping,
the constant fleeing
the horror creeping close behind,
as darkness descends.

Unlit courtyards drown
in the grey miasma of twilight;
heaped piles of tenement slums,
eyeless and threatening,
dingy hallways calling,
tattered curtains beckoning;

the low lap of a river
licking the days rubbish
from its dark, muddy gums.
Darkness, void; the phantom crowd
dissolving, slinking through the alleys
like rats frightened
by the stalking shadow of Night
creeping like an enormous black cat
across empty, drizzle slick streets;
all eyes, all faces, hands and bodies,
all vanished like cockroaches
fleeing the light, scurrying
into a thousand crooked cracks,
black puddles into which
whole buildings sink.
The silence of desertion,
darkness and the terror of wax
waiting for the flame to consume it;
the child is alone.

Distorted senses contort
every sound, every glimmer
of spectral light caught
in the corner of an eye,
every panicked cry answered
by demons crouching,
muttering just beyond sight,
just beyond the glow of yellow lamps
hanging like skulls, guttering, dieing,
great sighing beasts gathering
in the damp night, waiting
eyes narrowed, bright with cruel disdain
watching this child, this feast,
lost and alone in their fearful domain,
and so comes despair,
terror and madness.

Imagine now another child,
younger, more vulnerable,
impressionable, afraid,
lost in the grey immensity
of a shadow world,
a vast colourless monotony

beside which the arcades
of the deserted city shine
like pretty pearls.
Imagine the terror,
the helplessness, the crying,
the calling, the utter destruction of hope,
the appalling awareness
that this is real, no nightmare,
no waking here, only absolute fear
and the assurance of pain.

Trembling, hiding, weeping,
praying they are dreaming,
panicked flight and furtive creeping,
running again, then lying, screaming,
face pressed into the ground, gasping,
breathing the fetid air that shivers
with the final breath of those
lying bound upon the rack.
Mumbling prayers, stumbling
through endless ruin,
a fallen necropolis filled
with the cacophony of despair,
peopled by the suffering souls
of abandoned children
whose agonised screams spill
like curses from every blind
doorway punched
into the inner blackness
of crumbling mausoleums,
vaulted tombs stand
leering like paedophiles
in the shifting gloom.

This is the world of the damned.
Lost, lonely, afraid,
forever terrified
by the looming shape
of their own grotesque shadow,
their dark past hovering above them
like a predatory angel;
relentlessly haunted by a fear
greater than that of eternal loss,

far worse, the paralysing fear
of discovery. The fear that today,
this hour, this minute
they will be found by the terror
that follows, stalking, searching,
pursuing them without pause,
without rest, only one street away.
Cowering, praying, listening
as it calls their name
in a sweet, sickly voice
charged with foreboding,
feigning concern,
promising the caress of forgiveness
while whispering the curse of revenge

Staggering on, forever on,
trembling with dread,
suffering agonies of apprehension
with every intolerable, unending moment;
turning the head with each furtive step
to glimpse nothing
but knowing it is there
and all flight is futile,
knowing that soon it shall catch them,
seize them by the hand,
snatch them back with its sickening smile,
watery eyes and silken voice,
painted lips laced with poisonous kisses,
back into the loathsome, loveless bosom
of the dark, violent hell
that is their eternal home.

Dancer in a temple of doom

Eyes there are that cruel dwell
upon her bosoms naked swell
and lips that in a mocking grin
smile to see her body spin,
and mouths that utter whispers coarse,
and throats that laugh with humour hoarse,
and ears that catch her every sigh
and dare her wilting soul to die.
Hands that grip a spears shaft
or fondle the axe's polished haft,
as chained feet tap the rhythm droll
of drums that somewhere hidden roll,
and mouths that scream and pipes that sing,
bells that clang and hands that wring,
murmuring lips, crude and obscene,
with cymbals, and gongs and tambourines.
Tears falling through golden mesh.
the shivering flinch of naked flesh
at the perfumed touch of an iron fist
and nothing so cruel as the jailer's kiss,
or the cold caress of the scimitar's blade,
or the hot embrace of the iron maid.
The brush of a lip, the kiss of a boot,
a wail of joy, or agony mute,
the leer of a god carved in stone,
the gaze of eyes in gloom alone,
the dieing lovers masked embrace,
the innocent smile on a murderer's face
that offers comfort as she dances by,
with only Death in his cold blue eyes.
Muscles that strain, limbs that ache,
a fear that dare not make a mistake.
Failure will herald derision and pain,
and success the hell of dancing again.
A last pirouette, she falls to her knees,
a hand on her arm! Does it comfort or tease?

A Poole Fathom-lesse as I

A pool Fathomless as I
has not a Will to Live or Die;
beyond the Ripples upon my Face
spreads a Dark unending Space
that knows Nothing of the Passing Fears
of the Outer, transient Years.
For in the Waters of my Thought
Strange and Terrible Forms are caught,
Leviathans, locked from Light,
Haunt the Ether of my Night,
and Krakens dread to Human-eyes,
Frightening in their Awful size,
tentacle with saline Might
the Stars that Fall, fresh and Bright,
into the Silence of my Dream
where Restless Serpents coil and stream
and flow like Pennoncelles of Doom
spiralling through my Ageless Gloom;
and like Stones hapless hurled
by careless Hands from out the World
into a Mere or Restless Sea,
so Frightened Memories ripple me
and through my Endless Vortex sink,
like silver Coin they Flash and blink
into the Blackness wherein
their Light shall be Forever dimmed;
and some have only just begun
to Orbit around my Darkened Sun,
in the Upper-Deeps they fall like Rain
where Mighty Dragons heave and Strain
like Leaden Carp that Rise to feed
from their Bed of Plaited Weeds
upon the Crumbs that Fools throw
to Face a Terror they cannot Know;
and some have reached my Deeper Houses
where Silence like a Monster browses
upon the Hate that is His own,
Feasting in the Gloom alone.

And yet their sinking shall not cease,
nor Panicked Minds find any Peace,
indeed the Horrors shall Multiply
as Consciously the Depths drift by
where Suspended Worms of Dread
suck upon the Fearful Dead,
where undulates the Festering Leech
as dying Behemoths strive to reach
the Surface they shall never see
before sinking backwards steadily
once more into Oblivious Gloom
that is Forever their Lonely Tomb.
But though they drift through Countless Years
Down into my Sea of Tears
they shall never reach the Deeps
where I the Nameless Monster Sleep,
and no other Creatures Glide
through this the Blackest of my Tides,
for I alone can Know these Ways
Immeasurable and Endless as My Days
that Unnumbered stretch far back in Time,
before the Waking of the Slime
wherein the Sleeping Man was Borne
before he awoke to Life forlorn.
But even I may not know
what Darker Depths beneath me flow,
nor what Hand, for it was not Mine,
filled these Leagues Labyrinthine
and formed this Void of Starless Night
where Creatures wander without Sight,
nor whether yet more Dwell below
these Dull Arcades of Gloom I know,
and mayhap it is I do but drown,
as do the Thoughts that I call down,
within the Morass of a Mind
Vaster and more Dread than Mine.
But if beneath my Abyss lie
more Fiends I know they may not rise
lest I summon Them here to Me
and in this I show my Mastery.

So I Dream my Nightmare long
and prove Conjecture idle wrong
for none come to Me save at My Call,
I Exist alone, it is they Must Fall.
Yet sometimes when I Dreaming Sleep
and Ponder on some Horror Deep
a Touch shall wake Me from My Thought,
yet in the Darkness there is nought,
yet still I feel some Presence glide
close beneath my Sleeping side
and I am conscious of the Thought
that somehow even I am Caught
within a Web more Vast than Mine
that Anchors me in Space and Time.
Then it Frightens Me to think
that without pause I too Sink,
constant, down, Endless slow
into the icy Void below,
and even a Pool Fathomless as I
that has No Will to Live, may Die.

(Fragment in original form)

A poole Fathom-lesse as I
hast notte a Wille to Live or Dye;
beyond the Rypples upon my Fayce
spreades a Darke un-Ending Spayce
thatte knows Nothing of the Passing Feares
of the Outer, transyente Yeares.

The Ghoule.

Darkness cloaks the paths She walks,
gloom and mist shroud Her ways,
dim-light groping flecks the leaves
lying dead upon Her paths,
fighting, like a wounded knight
in frosted steel, it filters down
through tangled boughs
that gnarled and knotted
hang from crippled boles,
trembling as it feels the touch
of branches, heavy with lichen-lace,
that groan as down by degrees
through the Seasons they sink,
until the dull crack ends them
and sends them down to rot
in earth made rich
with their own children.
Strange weeds like cobras
coil amid the pale grass
that whispering lines
those ways, with tendrils
white as flesh they creep and knot,
binding tight the weave
of strangled stalks and broken stems,
damp and rank their wormlike roots
dig deep beside those
of the hunchbacked Oak
that deeper delves to twine,
with coils cold as ice,
the frightened dead.
Stones like Monoliths
moss cloaked rise,
grey ghosts ivy-coiled,
or lie, bramble-bound,
chained to the festering clay;
some like ancient Crags still stand
above the waste
their weathered features hard set,
defeat close upon them
as up the Night-shade climbs
slowly stifling the stone,

whilst beneath
terrible roots destroy the soil
about their base,
until one Midnight chime,
when mist like a phantom sea
breaks upon them and the stars,
like a crowd gathered
too see them die, stare down
with their one-eyed mistress,
whose pale orb,
pitiless and unblinking,
lights the stage
upon which this Tragedy
must play, the aged stones
leaning, straining, can stand no more
and crashing fall, afraid
into the waiting talons
of the bramble-claws
that wrap their prey
like Python coils,
until with Time,
when the half-grown fronds
full leaf, the stones are seen no more.

Here it is She moves,
where none dare stray
even in the Sun's strong light
and if the hapless Owl
chances too see
beneath his wing
the spectral stones,
those sepulchres of forgotten-Time,
arrayed like a grim army
of grey doom,
then hear his frighted shriek
as away like an arrow he hurls
with a horde of demon Bats
calling close behind.
Yet here it is She walks
and dares the Devil's horde,
and some say that She
the mistress of these Dark-Creatures
stands peerless in their sight,

though others whisper
that She is shunned
by those that Light and Life
have already cast out;
that even the friendless Fiends
will not endure Her company,
and the Demons howl
and for Pity cow,
and snarl for Fear
if She but extend
a comforting hand.
Who then is She
that hides from Day
and wraith-like
walks away the Darkness hours
amid mausoleums
and fractured tombs,
open vaults and rotting flowers?
and peeps into Moonlit crypts,
dark chasms of granite,
wherein the restless dead
sleep and Dream?
And why is it that She
appears in their Dreams
like a Phantasm
to haunt their frightful rest?
Why do they shudder
in their lead and pine,
and turn and moan
and sometimes cause
their caskets to crash
and splinter upon the cold stone,
to leave their naked bones
exposed too what dread Terror?
Who is She that enters Dark places
unknown to any that walk
the Daylight ways,
and practices rites
that all save She,
and the stones,
and the lifeless bones
have long forgot?

What moans and calls,
and sighs and sobs
surround Her where She goes?
Body cloaked, head cowled
in shadows too dark
too mark the features there,
that whispers say would, if seen,
turn the haughty Medusa
like a child to stone.
Who is She that weeps
when none may see,
tears that scorch like fire
Her pallid cheeks?
What bitter cries break
from deep within Her breast?
What Hatred without rest
stirs there in her secret heart?
What awful loathing
must cause those flames to flare
and spark from dark eyes
bright with a strange and terrible desire?
What cruel yearning,
burning in the Darkness,
draws such tears of sadness
from the well of pain
sunk so deep within her?
Yet bitter as those tears are
they cannot extinguish
the fires of madness and chaos
that glint and shine and die
in the lonely Ghoul's eyes?

(Fragment in original form)

Darknesse cloakes the pathes she walkes
gloome and miste shroude her wayes,
dim lyght gropeyng fleckes the leaves

The supplicant

The call is made, the words spoken,
an orison prayed to a god that never once
has stirred. A supplication sent into silence.
Ignored, or simply unheard? Yet he kneels
and yields up his words undeterred
by years of disappointment; all his hopes
voiced into the vast unknown, the void
into which have flown countless pleas,
the expectation wrapped within them
worn thin as the skin upon his knees.
Eyes and hands squeezed shut, heart open,
the muttered syllables broken, stuttering
from lips drawn in a grim line
across the anguished face.
The desperation, the heart-rending desire,
that trace of fear mixed with tears
and coloured with shades of fading hope
and growing dejection. The mind
fired by the will to wish the dream alive,
a will that struggles to survive
in the face of such rejection.
Tottering on the very brink
of despair. Anticipation eroded
by that serpent thought, that doubt,
that fear, that subtle, whispered curse
that far worse than the absence
of anyone there to hear,
yes, they hear, but do not care.

The violent dead

Time does not move upon these deeps,
this crystal Age in which they sleep,
nor can a tide this ocean shake
or from this shore these waters take,
and though some zephyr of passing years
may shiver the stars to frozen tears
it dare not tremble this hidden sea
where-in their ageless spirits keep
their silent vigil of slumbering joy
with no waking hour their bliss to cloy.

Not one second's passing sigh shall stir
the smallest curl of their golden hair,
nor any moment of Time depart
the long eternity of their quiet hearts;
for these spirits stand aloof from Time,
and live in an epoch of days sublime
and they do not measure with a mortal span
their endless nights remote from Man;
nor can they be moved by threat of years
who sleep apart from worldly fears,
no more touched by prayers, or tears.
For they have suffered and now they reap
the harvest of peace and dreamless sleep.

The Vampyre

He dreams
of vapours passing pale candles
wavering, trembling afraid
in hallways dim, obscure half-lit
and, drifting with the mist,
music, solemn and cold, lonely,
echoing in an endless,
soulless refrain, hollow voices
calling to a lost …?

He sees
doorways, dismal, dark,
half open to shadows
and through their flaking
oaken lips dull stairs
winding down, down into gloom,
where strange moans and murmurs
whisper a woe that cannot be eased,
cannot be silenced,
grieving for a lost …?

He envisions
vast labyrinthine catacombs,
dripping diamond beads,
icy tears sparking
in the flicker of a guttering torch
and away into the dark
footsteps receding deep,
deep into Stygian wastes,
lonely footfalls
fading into icy Oblivion,
seeking, ever seeking,
searching for a lost …?

He knows
only night, only darkness
unending, unbroken,
tangible in its blindness,
oppressive, filled with wandering forms
that weep and groan and sigh;
darkened eyes filled
with regret and accusation,
open mouths, strangely voiceless,
chant strange hymns,
prayers sung for forgiveness
sent into the blackness
without hope of response,
and he there amongst them
singing in hollow tones,
long and soft and low,
empty words, meaningless words
sounding all around him,
incantations booming, screaming,
echoing, then gone, lost,
simply lost.

The soldier

He only hoped that somehow
he might escape this fate,
might not be left behind to keep
this gate but flee with the others,
not too late, and live to see
his home and hold his wife
and children close and not leave them
alone to fend against the war
without a hope to see him smile
once more, as he yet hopes
that he might one day
see them again
and smile once more.

Macbeth Song

He stands on the shore
of a vast endless sea
throwing dreams at the waves
rushing on from the deep.

He calls to the wind
in a strange, foreign tongue
and the sad wind replies
with a low, lonely moan.

He tells his sad tale
to the clouds drifting by
as they race for the hills
on whose sides they must die.

He mimics the fall
of bright stars in a pool
and the sparks of their tears
paint his face like a fool.

He races the moon
over dark, lonely sands,
turning the tide
with the sweep of his hands.

He screams with the gale
from his black mental cage,
and it lashes his soul
with its blind, mindless rage.

He trips on bright rainbows
falling down with the rain
and the drops dance upon him
like diamonds of pain.

Woman

She sits beside the window the cold light
fading the colour from her face,
staring into nothing as a woman might
who has spent the night upon the shore
listening to the thunder roar
and felt the sting of rain and hail
as the heaving surf forced on by the gale
crashed and smashed against the harbour wall,
as she called into the violent pall of night
and searched in vain for her husband's light
amid the wailing squall
that with the passing of the storm
slowly screamed itself to sleep
and left her drained of hope
to weep and keep her vigil upon the wall
as night passed into feeble dawn
that paled the grey of sky and sea,
and still no mast nor flag to see
on the misty horizon,
only widowed weed upon the swell
that breathed as though in sleep
beneath a vast brawl of rolling cloud,
each scudding shade melting
into a single shroud, vague and grey
and empty, the colour of drowned flesh,
as gulls wheeled and cried,
and small waves chafed and sighed
against the pebbled shore,
urged on by a mournful breeze,
fresh and cold as a breath escaped
from the House of Death.
So from her the last belief ebbed away
and she grieved for a love
that would come no more,
as a stave of wood
painted black as jet
knocked against the harbour wall
like Fate upon a door
and so to home, alone.

Grief

He said, 'There is a land of grief,
set apart from all belief,
where souls wander to and fro
and cry their bitter tears of woe
and weep against the silent skies
the mad profanities of their eyes'.
She smiled and said, 'I know a place
where Cruelty walks without a face
whilst Pity, like a lame dog led,
upon her master's deeds is fed
until the whining, glutted beast
attracts his blows and joins the feast'.
He sighed, 'There is a realm, a shadow land,
where angels still as tombstones stand
transfixed and watch without reply
as helpless souls for mercy cry
whilst Evil, great as any god,
breaks them with his iron rod'.
She laughed and said, 'I know a land of dreams
where nothing is real nor as it seems,
it borders a land of brutal reality
where suffering is seen with absolute clarity
by all the dreamers who watching still
consume each atrocity with a guilty thrill'.
He sadly said, 'I no longer wish to live
in a world were deceitful smiles give
no hint of the pain they wilfully hide
and shattered lives, like tears, slide
into oblivion. Where is the land where one can be,
if not happy, then spared such desperate misery?'
She only sneered and said, 'I know that land,
where people go without a single strand
of what they have known, have seen,
have shared, have felt, have been,
ever following them there; where all is still
and they stare into great black pools filled
with tears unshed, and guilt and shame,
and words unsaid, terrible regrets and pain,
and lament in silence as they await in dread
He that stalks the Land of the Dead!'

The Captive Saracen

I am a demon;
my heart is black and cold,
unfeeling. I am less than other men
yet greater than most
for though they revile me
as they would a dog
they fear me as they would a wolf.
My passions are all of hate
and my dark eyes burn with fires
they cannot understand.
I speak in a tongue
they cannot comprehend
and say it is the language of the damned.
Damned indeed, to the fire
that reflects in their eyes
with its stake and chains
and I shall curse and call
and they shall count my screams
as the ravings of a soul lost.
Yet the terror of my curse
shall ring through their years
and they shall fear to die
lest in that deeper darkness
they meet with me again,
as I pray they do,
for to their imagining
I am a demon.

Upon the vampyr's eyes

See his midnight curve of eye,
a lightless vacuum jellified,
liquefied, a starless void,
light-denied, frozen
in an ageless state,
an orb of midnight,
polished hate,
an abyss-drawn drop
of blackest pitch, or ripened berry
of poison picked by a blind witch,
demon-slave of darkness,
in a dripping cave where phantom's
lost in horror rave;
yet behind their glint of unfired coal
reflects the anguish of a soul
chained where no hint of light
nor word of hope can ever console.
And the stars that fall through timeless space
across his eyes strange patterns trace,
like fleeting ghosts of past regrets
etched on a surface of polished jet,
or new moons that rise and lightless set
yet leave upon those inky spheres
a sheen of long forgotten tears,
falling, crawling, tortured-tears
that carved these orbs like glacial ice,
with runes of woe that mark the price,
paid and paid again,
the price of pride, the price of shame
engraved upon these lightless,
lifeless, tearless eyes.

The Fallen

There is no mark
of Chaos on his brow.
No line of stern desire
thwarted in its last exertion
mars his parted lips.
A blanche of fatigue,
that's all, seems to weary
the fading colour of his cheek,
but better this than a passionate lust
frozen in it's purple shame.

See how calm the eyes,
like pools filmed with a cold dawn's frost,
stare into the clouding sky
as if in contemplation of the quiet still
of which he is now a part,
gazing unconcerned
upon the gathering storm
he need not fear.
No wild glare of anger
emptied from a troubled soul
into a fevered eye;
no look of disdain for this world,
the fire damped
in the cooling grate of Death.
No twisted brow stamped with rage,
or nostril blown with a snarling hate;
an aged child he seems
caught, as often mothers' catch their boys,
not in mischief's way
but in a wistful, pensive play,
wonder rapt in a world of manly deeds,
their budding manhood checked
not by the courage to do,
but by the ignorance of how.

He does not lie alone
and yet upon this patch of ground
that is his own he is as lonely now
as ever boy or man can be,
one of a company of lonely men
whose comradeship here
no time nor test can break.
He is one of those elite,
whose warrior skills
have earned for him
the highest, yet coldest of all rewards,
the Immortal Memory.
Not for him the sad return
to lands forsaken for the sword,
lands filled with sad looks,
recrimination and guilt.
Not for him the tearful homecoming
soon forgot in daily toil,
routine restored
and the attentions of those that nod
but cannot know
the things he cannot tell.
Not for him the winter's age
when his memory speaks a tale
that all save he has long forgot
or grown bored of in the telling.

No, for him now the ballad sung
in palace hall and village inn,
for a timeless age remembered
in a hymn of thanksgiving.
For him a name to turn the lips of men
to smile as they, in pretence of memory,
remember him as a friend, a hero,
a model of their kind
that all should revere and know.
For him the absolution of Death;
all past ills and wrongs
forgotten and forgiven,
his live deeds enhanced
by tongues that speak only good
of him that fell.

Until indeed he lives in mind
a better man than ever left his home
to carry arms against a foe
that those behind could never face or know.
An example for generations yet unborn
to hold in awe and high esteem,
to be looked upon across great gulfs of Time
as a shining show of what a man should be,
once was and is no more.
Until Time shall despair of his fame
and think "Is this the man that I saw slain?"

But far in his dead future lies the legend
that now is just a man
who bleeding sleeps upon this field,
and somewhere in his frozen present
a wife shall wake to mourn,
and children to weep,
not knowing that their grief is premature
for this man has yet to be reborn,
shall yet live in myth,
a hero for all time.

The Odalisque

If you dare the severing blade
and oriental skills of him
who lives and works
demon-like in darkness
there in wells of unfathomed Night,
within dark vaults concealed,
sweet scented with the odour of blood,
fresh and congealed,
where empty echoes of pain
carry despair through every reach
of that dark labyrinthine world,
where tormented shadows scream,
condemned to live a nightmare
between the crushing jaws of an iron Death
until the last of life and breath
is torn and rent from their fibred flesh
by him, the deaf Malach,
who spider-like waits
for the web of silk that clothes
in perfumed mist the harem walls,
to draw easy prey to his dark feast
beneath tulip-minarets
with golden lotus domes
that rise on slender stalks,
polished white as the passing fleece
of bright clouds that sail by
through azure deeps,
like wandering Sinbads,
innocent of the fear
that never sleeps below.

If you dare this,
the cold blade's kiss,
and lie still and cold
beside flamingos pink
and fish of gold, that move
like stately phantoms
amid the lily pads
that carpet the silent pool

shadowed by a marble arch
that spans its dark-mirror -
from quarter to quarter
of this exquisite tomb -
a bridge of sighs,
aptly named, for death of spirit
and loss of hope lie close by
on feathered divans,
close to the shining scimitar's
winking eye, held by him,
the evil, dark Malach;

then wait and you may see her pass,
faery-like, a soft apparition
glimpsed through pastel panes,
framed in the peacock portals
that pierce the span with arabesques
of jewelled light, and,
if your dreams be true,
she may pause, like a moth
beside a dieing flame,
to watch distracted
the sudden sheen of a carp
swimming heavy plated by
within that glass wherein
she sees her own small face
caged in splendour reflect,
and perhaps, as many times before,
she shall weep and sigh
her crystal tears
like falling gems
rippling the waters
that hold you, trembling,
rapt with awe.

Then quickly, drink deep
the absinthe of her eyes
for pause she may for only a few
brief, fleeting beats of her racing heart
upon the petal-strewn alabaster
of the paved walk that leads
her steps from one chiffon confine
to another, equally splendid,

equally confined;
study her peerless features,
the flawless skin,
the sad, lustrous eyes
her soft, honeyed lips,
and read there the woe that began
ten times ten centuries ago
when a woman-child like she
was born into an age of barbarity,
stolen in her youth
for the beauty of her face
and the grace of her limbs,
bought, sold, gifted,
to live as a concubine,
a slave to salve the whim
of some savage lord
that held with fear
the fealty of her people,
and now, sad centuries later,
she, though not in tents of hide,
or packed, carpet-like,
upon a camel's back,
or struggling for dignity and life
upon some burning dune,
is yet as much a slave, if not more,
in these halls of pearl and ebony
embalmed like a living mummy
in scented silks;
carried like an icon,
if abroad she must,
lest her perfect feet should cloy
with common dust,
within a sedan of cedar and gold,
borne by slaves bound
with silver chains,
eyes blinkered lest they
behold even her foot
as she steps on silver cushions
into their charge;

more a possession than ever
her captive ancestor was
who at least fell prey
to a warrior's lust,
and did not have to bear
the touch of a perfumed despot,
or petulant child-prince,
spoiled and cruel,
or aged tyrant, rheumy eyed
a drooling fool;
nor was she hard won,
defended to the death
by fearless kin, booty
of some bloody fight,
but sold to her oppressor,
a weakling in his dotage,
a tribute of living flesh,
a mindless toy to satisfy
the puppet-pleasures
of a senile lord whose attentions
appal and slobbering whims
and fancies disgust.

A child still it is that gazes down,
like a bewildered nymph
who wishes the waters nearer
that she may leap and swim
forever with the golden carp
in the cool oblivion of those depths
at peace, wrapped in a lily shroud,
but in her experienced, aged mind
it is a woman that thinks on death,
a woman of flesh and intelligence
that reflects on wasted, wasting time,
her life a living crime of passing years
that must one day bring to her
only ridicule and scorn,
and a cruel death at the hands of him,
the cruel Malach,
an end, of sorts,
for her who now has gone
and passed from view,
for her, the odalisque.

Nightmare 1

Darkness brings the soul's lust;
pain and woe his want must bring.
"Not so close! Please, alone!"
and shakes the sudden sob
wrung from the beating heart
by the proximity of the terrible Fate
that waits in darkened rooms
where his feet must tread,
though heavy as lead, alone.

Wide and white the eyes that straining
seek him in his trembling. A groan
in the darkness, the quivering tone
of all hope draining away,
of complete spiritual defeat.
Cries that echo in barren halls,
empty doors and narrow walls
surround him. Who hides there
in the shadowed soul
and stalks the dark bound mind
lurching blind behind his sight?

Fear turns the oblivion of night
into an endless tunnel of horror
in whose impenetrable recesses
tormented daemons hide,
their twisted faces invisible, but there.

"Away a little pace! Oh peace!"
Final terror draws the heavy gasp
unconscious from the quaking breast,
and the mind is startled into deeper fear
by the volume of the breath.

The man who walks through life
with Death in his heart
is already dead.

Time will pass

Time will pass
but I remain
always the same,
I stand-alone
above the common herd
of dieing men
and watch them as they fall,
answering some primeval call
that lures them into eternity
with the promise of an easy paradise.
Ah! dream of dreams
that it were true,
for me no more than them,
that I may join
their mad flight from life
and leave this world,
a cinder in a dieing fire,
far behind.
But this is not to be
and I must stay
whilst others go,
while all else goes.

The Odalisque iii

"You are my prisoner", and turning she
caught in his eye such cruelty
that spoke her station in his heart
a love to have and to hold apart;
a love to taste when others failed
and sweeter fruits turn old and stale;
a love to drink when the well is dry
and the tears all shed in another's eye;
a love to touch when idle arms
weary of another's charms;
and a love to hurt knowing that she
from cruel attentions cannot flee.

"You are my slave", and sighing she
caught in his tone such mastery
that spoke the pride that choked his heart
and held him in his mind apart
from all others who for him
lived only to serve his every whim.
A thing that wealth he had not earned
had bought for him when his passion burned
and flames of lust ran through his veins,
to have this girl, alone, in chains,
knowing that she may not withhold
the body purchased for a piece of gold.

What was he like

What was he like?
A ship becalmed
on a voyage to shores
that called for discovery,
lying horizon fast,
unable to sail those last
few leagues to see
what waited there.
A sailor marooned
on an island of plenty
whose hopes of rescue
seemed perverse
in the eyes of those
marooned with him
in paradise.
A vessel moored
to the unyielding quay
whilst the fleet,
full sailed turns for the sea
leaving its barnacled keel
stranded, sails furled,
compass covered,
empty hold and charts
open but unseen
waiting masterless
in the cabin's gloom.
A man, with every opportunity,
who stayed ashore
as his fellows signed articles
and seaward sped,
as if waiting to be pressed,
waiting for that compelling invitation
that all the time he kept
pocketed and unread.

Index of first lines